Landform Top Tens

The World's Most Amazing Coasts

Anna Claybourne

Chicago, Illinois

www.heinemannraintree.com
Visit our website to find out more information about Heinemann-Raintree books.

To order:
☎ Phone 888-454-2279
💻 Visit www.heinemannraintree.com to browse our catalog and order online.

Edited by Louise Galpine, Kate DeVilliers, and Rachel Howells
Designed by Victoria Bevan and Geoff Ward
Original illustrations © Capstone Global Library Limited
Illustrated by Geoff Ward
Picture research by Hannah Taylor
Production by Alison Parsons

Printed in China by CTPS

13 12 11 10 09
10 9 8 7 6 5 4 3 2 1

Library of Congress Cataloging-in-Publication Data

Claybourne, Anna.
  The world's most amazing coasts / Anna Claybourne.
    p. cm. -- (Landform top tens)
  Includes bibliographical references and index.
  ISBN 978-1-4109-3699-8 (hc) -- ISBN 978-1-4109-3707-0 (pb)
  1. Coasts--Juvenile literature. I. Title.
  GB453.C53 2008
  551.45'7--dc22
                          2008051493

Acknowledgments

We would like to thank the following for permission to reproduce photographs: Ardea.com pp. **8** (Francois Gohier), **13** and **20** (Jean Paul Ferrero); Corbis p. **14** (Michael T. Sedam); FLPA pp. **12** (Minden Pictures/ Fred Bavendam), **25** (Winfried Wisniewski); National Geographic Stock pp. **18** and **19** (Paul Zahl); naturepl p. **11** (Ashok Jain); photographersdirect.com p. **6** (Paulo Backes Photography); Photolibrary pp. **4–5** (Robert Harding Travel/ Christopher Nicholson), **9** (Creatas), **15** (Pacific Stock/ Joe Carini), **16** (Cusp/ Theo Allofs), **17** (Robert Harding Travel/ Thorsten Milse), **21** (Mark A Johnson), **24** (Cusp/ Wolfgang Meier), **26** (OSF/ Warren Faidley), **27** (Corbis); shutterstock p. **23** (Pavel Dunyushkin); Still Pictures p. **10** (Majority World/ Mustafiz Mumun); Tips Images p. **22**; Eduardo Tavares_JC/ BrazilPhotos p. **7**.

Background images by Photodisc.

Cover photograph of the cliffs of Molokai, Hawaii, reproduced with permission of Photolibrary (Pacific Stock/ Ron Dahlquist).

We would like to thank Nick Lapthorn for his invaluable help in the preparation of this book.

Every effort has been made to contact copyright holders of material reproduced in this book. Any omissions will be rectified in subsequent printings if notice is given to the publishers.

Disclaimer

All the Internet addresses (URLs) given in this book were valid at the time of going to press. However, due to the dynamic nature of the Internet, some addresses may have changed, or sites may have changed or ceased to exist since publication. While the author and publishers regret any inconvenience this may cause readers, no responsibility for any such changes can be accepted by either the author or the publishers. It is recommended that adults supervise children on the Internet.

Contents

Some words are printed in bold, **like this**. You can find out what they mean by looking in the glossary on page 31.

Coasts

Coasts are places where the land meets the sea. Earth is broken up into seven huge sections called **continents**. There are also thousands of smaller islands. All these pieces of land are surrounded by sea. Altogether, the world has over 1.6 million kilometers (1 million miles) of **coastline**.

There are many different types of coasts. Many coastlines also have amazing features, such as tower-like **sea stacks**, sea caves, and rock arches, or wildlife such as **mangrove** forests and **coral reefs**.

Changing coasts

All coastlines change over time. The action of wind, waves, and storms **erodes** some parts of the coast. In other places, the sea **deposits** sand and mud on the coast, making it grow.

Coasts and us

Coasts are incredibly important for human beings. We use the sea for fishing, carrying cargo, and having fun. Many of the world's cities, towns, and villages are close to the sea. They were built there because being by the coast made it easier for people to travel, deliver goods, and make a living by fishing. Today, coastal towns and cities often make money from tourists.

Durdle Door in Dorset, England, is a coastal arch. Waves have worn a hole through the rock, creating a bridge shape.

Praia do Cassino

Praia do Cassino, or Cassino Beach, is the world's longest sandy beach. It stretches from the city of Rio Grande to Brazil's border with Uruguay. Like many sandy beaches, it is popular with surfers and vacationers. It is wide and flat, with pale golden sand.

This aerial photograph gives an idea of how long Cassino Beach is.

PRAIA DO CASSINO

LOCATION:
BRAZIL, SOUTH AMERICA

TYPE OF COASTLINE:
SANDY BEACH

LENGTH:
240 KM (150 MILES)

HOW IT FORMED:
BREAKING WAVES **DEPOSITED** GRAINS OF SAND ON THE SHORE

THAT'S AMAZING!
CASSINO BEACH CONTINUES TO GROW AS THE WAVES DEPOSIT MORE SAND ALONG THE **COASTLINE**.

SOUTH AMERICA

Pacific Ocean

Atlantic Ocean

Praia do Cassino

Fishermen haul in their nets on Cassino Beach.

Beach-building

Sandy beaches are made by waves. As waves crash against rocks, they wear them away. They gradually **erode** (wear down) the rock into tiny **grains** of sand. Where waves break onto flatter parts of the coast, they leave grains of sand behind. Gradually, more and more sand collects, forming a beach.

Space for science

Scientists love Cassino Beach. The huge amounts of space along its sandy shore make it easier for them to study the coast. They study the waves, sand movements, and sea and beach wildlife.

The Bay of Fundy

The Bay of Fundy in Canada has the biggest **tidal range** in the world. That means it has the biggest difference in water level between **high tide** and **low tide**—up to 17 meters (56 feet), or as high as a five-floor building! At most coasts, the difference is only about 3 meters (10 feet).

Harbors in the Bay of Fundy have to be built very high, to allow for the extra-high tides.

BAY OF FUNDY

LOCATION:
CANADA, NORTH AMERICA

TYPE OF COASTLINE:
BAY

LENGTH:
290 KM (180 MILES)

HOW IT FORMED:
SEAWATER FILLED A DEEP RIFT VALLEY BETWEEN TWO AREAS OF LAND

THAT'S AMAZING!
AT HIGH TIDE, THE SEA RUSHES INTO RIVERS AROUND THE BAY, MAKING THEM FLOW BACKWARD.

NORTH AMERICA

Pacific Ocean

Bay of Fundy

Deep waters

The Bay of Fundy formed long ago, as the sections of land that make up Earth's **continents** gradually broke apart. This created a long, deep valley, called a rift valley, that filled up with seawater.

The **tides** stir up water from the depths of the bay. It is filled with **nutrients**. Tiny sea creatures called **plankton** feed on them, and whales come to feed on the plankton. You can spot 15 types of whale in the Bay of Fundy.

At high tide, the water reaches as high as the plants on these rock pillars.

The Sundarbans

The Sundarbans lies on the border between India and Bangladesh, at the **mouth** of the Ganges River. It is the world's biggest **mangrove** forest. Mangroves are unusual trees that grow at the coast with their roots in the seawater. They have **adapted** to survive the changing **tides** and salty sea.

This typical Sundarbans landscape has low, muddy islands and slow-moving waterways.

THE SUNDARBANS

LOCATION:
INDIA AND BANGLADESH, ASIA

TYPE OF COASTLINE:
MANGROVE FOREST

AREA:
10,000 KM² (3,680 SQ MILES)

HOW IT FORMED:
MANGROVE TREES GREW AROUND THE SWAMPY ISLANDS FORMED BY THE GANGES **DELTA**

THAT'S AMAZING!
TIGERS IN THE SUNDARBANS KILL AT LEAST 25 PEOPLE EVERY YEAR.

ASIA

Pacific Ocean

Sundarbans

Indian Ocean

Fishermen in the Sundarbans sometimes wear masks on the backs of their heads to scare away hungry tigers.

Soggy Sundarbans

The Sundarbans area is made up of lots of small islands and swampy river channels. The land is very good for growing crops such as rice, so lots of people live there. The rivers, swamps, and mangroves also provide homes for all kinds of water wildlife.

The Great Barrier Reef

The Great Barrier Reef is the world's biggest **coral reef** system. It runs along the northeastern coast of Australia. It is made up of a long string of coral reefs and islands. It is famous for its warm, clear waters and amazing wildlife.

World of wildlife

Lots of sea creatures live around coral reefs. The Great Barrier Reef's wildlife includes sea turtles, giant clams, dolphins, sea snakes, sharks, dugongs (sea cows), and clownfish.

The Great Barrier Reef attracts lots of tourists, who go diving to view the coral and amazing sea creatures.

Pacific
Ocean

AUSTRALASIA

**Great
Barrier
Reef**

AUSTRALIA

What is a coral reef?

Coral reefs are made of a shell-like substance called coral. They are built in the sea by tiny sea creatures called **coral polyps**. When they die, they leave the coral behind, and new polyps build new coral on top. Over time, a coral reef grows and grows. It forms huge underwater platforms and caves, as well as islands.

This aerial photograph shows the Great Barrier Reef from the air.

The Cliffs of Molokai

Molokai is one of the islands that make up Hawaii. It has some of the highest sea cliffs in the world. At the village of Kalaupapa, the green, plant-covered cliffs are higher than the world's tallest skyscrapers.

The island of Molokai was formed by volcanoes on the seabed growing up out of the sea. Experts think half of one of these volcanoes fell into the sea in a giant **landslide**. The other half was left standing, with its steep slopes leading down to the sea.

The cliffs of Molokai tower over the seashore at Kalaupapa.

THE CLIFFS OF MOLOKAI

LOCATION:
HAWAII, NORTH AMERICA

TYPE OF COASTLINE:
CLIFFS

HEIGHT:
1,000 METERS (3,280 FEET)

HOW THEY FORMED:
A LANDSLIDE SLICED A VOLCANO IN HALF

THAT'S AMAZING!
SINCE THE CLIFFS AT MOLOKAI AREN'T COMPLETELY **VERTICAL**, YOU CAN CLIMB DOWN THEM ALONG A NARROW PATH.

NORTH AMERICA

Pacific Ocean

Atlantic Ocean

Cliffs of Molokai

Giant waterfall

Where streams flow over the edge of the cliffs, they form spectacular waterfalls. The tallest is called Kahiwa Falls. It is made up of a series of waterfalls that drop a total of 660 meters (2,165 feet) from the cliff tops into the sea.

The Skeleton Coast

Namibia's Skeleton Coast is a desert **coastline**, where giant sand dunes lie right up to the sea. It is part of the Namib Desert in southwest Africa and is one of the driest coasts anywhere in the world.

This shipwreck is now on dry land, because the shoreline has gradually moved away from it.

AFRICA

Indian Ocean

Atlantic Ocean

The Skeleton Coast

Deserts by the sea

Desert coasts are very rare. Deserts usually form in the middle of big **continents**, not by the sea. But off the coast of Namibia, there is a very cold **current** in the Atlantic Ocean. It means that water from the sea does not rise up high into the sky and form clouds, so there is very little rain.

This Namib Desert beetle is collecting a drink from the Skeleton Coast fog.

Drinking fog

Animals living along the Skeleton Coast must be able to cope with extremely dry conditions. The Namib Desert beetle lets the fog collect on its body as tiny drops of water. Then it lifts its body up to tip the water into its mouth.

Bioluminescent Bay

Bioluminescent Bay (also called Mosquito Bay) is in Puerto Rico, an island in the Caribbean Sea. It is the world's brightest glowing bay. If you paddle a kayak or swim there at night, the water glows with light! This happens because of tiny **bioluminescent plankton** that live in the water. When they are touched, they give out a burst of light. Scientists think this helps them to avoid being eaten by other sea creatures.

These are the plankton that make the water in Bioluminescent Bay glow.

BIOLUMINESCENT BAY

LOCATION:
PUERTO RICO,
NORTH AMERICA

TYPE OF COASTLINE:
BAY

AREA:
ABOUT 2 KM² (0.8 SQ MILES)

HOW IT FORMED:
A DEEP BAY FORMED BY WATER **EROSION**, FILLED UP WITH GLOWING PLANKTON

THAT'S AMAZING!
A CUPFUL OF WATER FROM THE BAY CONTAINS ABOUT 70,000 GLOWING PLANKTON!

NORTH AMERICA

Atlantic Ocean

Pacific Ocean

Bioluminescent Bay

Mangrove trees cover Bioluminescent Bay.

Why aren't all bays like this?

Bioluminescent Bay has a special set of features that help glowing plankton to survive. **Mangrove** trees around the bay release chemicals that the plankton feed on. The shape of the bay, which is deep with a narrow entrance, keeps the water cool enough for the plankton and stops them all from washing out to sea.

Ball's Pyramid

Ball's Pyramid is an amazing sight. It is a triangular spike of rock sticking straight up out of the sea off the coast of Lord Howe Island, Australia. Its coast is made of sheer rock plunging straight into the waves.

Ball's Pyramid is the remains of an ancient volcano that once stood in the same spot. Sea wind and waves **eroded** it and carved its sides, leaving the very narrow, sharp needle of rock behind.

You can go on a tour to view Ball's Pyramid from a boat or from the air.

BALL'S PYRAMID

LOCATION:
AUSTRALIA, **AUSTRALASIA**

TYPE OF COASTLINE:
ISLAND PINNACLE

HEIGHT:
552 METERS (1,811 FEET)

HOW IT FORMED:
WAVES AND WIND ERODED AN OLD VOLCANO

THAT'S AMAZING!
IN 2001, SCIENTISTS FOUND A STICK INSECT THAT THEY THOUGHT WAS **EXTINCT** LIVING ON BALL'S PYRAMID.

Who was Ball?

Ball's Pyramid is named after English explorer and navy captain Henry Lidgbird Ball. He discovered the pyramid, along with nearby Lord Howe Island, in 1788.

AUSTRALASIA

Pacific Ocean

Indian Ocean

AUSTRALIA

Ball's Pyramid

The jagged **coastline** of Lord Howe Island is the nearest land to Ball's Pyramid.

Curonian Spit

The Curonian **Spit**, on the border between Russia and Lithuania, is one of the world's biggest spits. It is a long, thin strip of sandy land covered in sand dunes (heaps of sand), including the highest moving sand dunes in Europe.

Some spits are very small, but the Curonian Spit is so big it has space for roads and towns on it. Lots of tourists visit its beaches in summer.

Vacationers flock to the Curonian Spit's beaches. There are concerns that this is spoiling the area's natural beauty.

CURONIAN SPIT

LOCATION:
RUSSIA AND LITHUANIA, EUROPE

TYPE OF COASTLINE:
SPIT

LENGTH:
98 KM (61 MILES)

HOW IT FORMED:
WIND AND WAVES CARRIED SAND OUT INTO THE SEA

THAT'S AMAZING!
THE CURONIAN SPIT HAS EXISTED FOR ABOUT 5,000 YEARS, DESPITE BEING UNDER CONSTANT THREAT FROM WIND AND WAVE **EROSION**.

Norwegian Sea

Curonian Spit

EUROPE

The sand dunes on the Curonian Spit can be as high as 60 meters (200 feet) tall.

What makes a spit?

Spits are formed when waves roll onto the shore, **depositing** sand. Sometimes the wind blows the waves along the shore as well. When this happens, the sand is moved along the beach and piles up at one end. This can create a sticking-out section of beach that gradually gets longer and longer. The area of sea trapped behind the spit is called a **lagoon**.

The Norwegian Fjords

Norway has an incredibly long, jagged (uneven) **coastline**. It is made of thousands of deep, narrow, finger-shaped sections of sea surrounded by land. They are called **fjords**. Norway has some of the world's longest, deepest, and most famous fjords. For example, Sognefjord is the longest and deepest fjord in Norway, at 203 km (126 miles) long and 1,308 meters (4,291 feet) deep.

Norway's fjords have very steep sides and are surrounded by towering cliffs.

Carved by ice

The fjords were created thousands of years ago, when Earth was much colder than it is now. Norway's mountains were covered with **glaciers**—huge rivers of ice that move slowly downhill to the sea. As they moved, the glaciers carved deep channels in the land. When Earth grew warmer and the ice melted, these channels were filled with seawater.

THE NORWEGIAN FJORDS

LOCATION:
NORWAY, EUROPE

TYPE OF COASTLINE:
FJORDS

LENGTH:
OVER 1,600 KM
(994 MILES)

HOW IT FORMED:
GLACIERS CARVED DEEP
CHANNELS THAT FILLED
UP WITH SEAWATER

THAT'S AMAZING!
THOUGH NORWAY IS
ONLY ABOUT 1,700 KM
(1,056 MILES) LONG, ITS JAGGED
COASTLINE IS OVER 25,000 KM
(15,534 MILES) LONG!

Norwegian
Sea

**Norwegian
Fjords**

EUROPE

The white-tailed eagle is a bird of prey that hunts for fish around the fjords.

Coasts in Danger

Many coastal areas are in danger from human activities. For example, rain and rivers can wash **pollution,** such as farm chemicals, from the land into the sea. This can make beaches dirty and poison seashore wildlife. Building cities and harbors on seashores destroys natural **habitats** where animals live, such as **mangrove** forests.

Another big problem for coasts is **global warming**—the way pollution in the air is making Earth warm up. Scientists think the warmer temperatures are damaging **coral reefs**. Global warming also causes more storms. These storms batter the coast, damage wildlife, and cause floods. Warmer weather also melts Earth's ice and makes the sea rise higher. This could flood many low-lying coasts and islands.

Hurricanes are big windstorms that blow onto the shore. Warmer weather makes them happen more often.

Coastal **erosion** is the wearing away of land by the sea. The Pacific Ocean has eroded the land beneath these houses.

What can we do?

Some countries protect their coasts by making areas of the seashore into national parks. Wildlife is protected from hunters, and people are not allowed to build new towns. The Sundarbans, for example, has been made into a national park. To protect the wildlife, it has some areas where no fishing is allowed, and guards throughout the forest watch for **poachers** (illegal hunters).

Coast Facts and Figures

Coasts come in many different shapes and sizes. Some are sandy playgrounds where people go on vacation. Others have steep cliffs, stormy waves, or stunning rock sculptures. Which **coastline** do you think is the most amazing?

This map of the world shows all the coasts described in this book.

Arctic Ocean

Norwegian Fjords

Curonian Spit

ASIA

NORTH AMERICA Bay of Fundy

EUROPE

Cliffs of Molokai

Bioluminescent Bay

AFRICA

Sundarbans

Pacific Ocean

SOUTH AMERICA

Atlantic Ocean

Indian Ocean

AUSTRALASIA Great Barrier Reef

Pacific Ocean

The Skeleton Coast

Ball's Pyramid

Praia do Cassino

Southern Ocean

ANTARCTICA

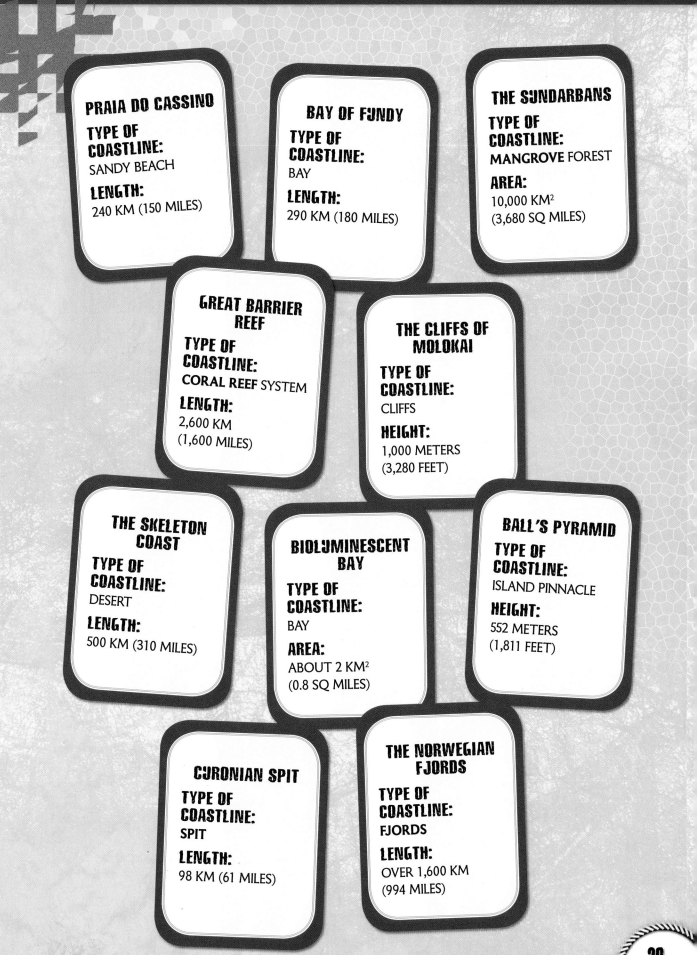

PRAIA DO CASSINO

TYPE OF COASTLINE:
SANDY BEACH

LENGTH:
240 KM (150 MILES)

BAY OF FUNDY

TYPE OF COASTLINE:
BAY

LENGTH:
290 KM (180 MILES)

THE SUNDARBANS

TYPE OF COASTLINE:
MANGROVE FOREST

AREA:
10,000 KM² (3,680 SQ MILES)

GREAT BARRIER REEF

TYPE OF COASTLINE:
CORAL REEF SYSTEM

LENGTH:
2,600 KM (1,600 MILES)

THE CLIFFS OF MOLOKAI

TYPE OF COASTLINE:
CLIFFS

HEIGHT:
1,000 METERS (3,280 FEET)

THE SKELETON COAST

TYPE OF COASTLINE:
DESERT

LENGTH:
500 KM (310 MILES)

BIOLUMINESCENT BAY

TYPE OF COASTLINE:
BAY

AREA:
ABOUT 2 KM² (0.8 SQ MILES)

BALL'S PYRAMID

TYPE OF COASTLINE:
ISLAND PINNACLE

HEIGHT:
552 METERS (1,811 FEET)

CURONIAN SPIT

TYPE OF COASTLINE:
SPIT

LENGTH:
98 KM (61 MILES)

THE NORWEGIAN FJORDS

TYPE OF COASTLINE:
FJORDS

LENGTH:
OVER 1,600 KM (994 MILES)

Find Out More

Books to read

Bowman, Lucy. *Usborne Beginners: Seashore.*
Tulsa, Okla.: EDC, 2008.

Green, Jen. *Geography Now!: Coastlines Around the World.*
New York: PowerKids, 2009.

Morris, Neil. *Landscapes and People: Earth's Changing Coasts.*
Chicago: Raintree, 2004.

Waldron, Melanie. *Mapping Earthforms: Coasts.*
Chicago: Heinemann Library, 2008.

Websites

Coral Reef Animal Printouts
www.enchantedlearning.com/biomes/coralreef/coralreef
This web page features pictures of lots of the animals that
can be found on coral reefs, along with useful facts.

Coral Reef Photobank
www.coral.org/resources/photobank
This web page has a gallery of beautiful images of coral
reefs and their wildlife from around the world.

Estuaries.gov
www.estuaries.gov
This website is all about estuaries (river mouths).

Glossary

adapt change over time to suit the surroundings

Australasia term used to describe Australia, New Zealand, and a series of nearby islands in the Pacific Ocean

bioluminescent living things that can glow with light

coastline border between the land and the sea

continent continuous land mass

coral polyp soft-bodied sea creature

coral reef underwater structure made of layers of coral

current flow of water

delta triangle-shaped area of islands and river channels where a river meets the sea

deposit drop or put down

erode wear away

extinct when a species has died out and no longer exists

fjord long, narrow, deep area of sea surrounded by land

glacier river of ice that flows slowly down a mountain

global warming gradual warming of Earth, caused by pollution

grain tiny piece of rock that makes up sand

habitat where a plant or animal lives

high tide highest point that seawater reaches as it is moved by the tide

lagoon area of sea cut off or almost cut off by a spit

landslide large fall of rocks and soil down the side of a mountain

low tide lowest point that seawater reaches as it is moved by the tide

mangrove type of tree that lives in salty water at the coast

mouth opening where a river flows into the sea

nutrient food chemical

plankton tiny sea creatures

poacher person who hunts where hunting is banned by law

pollution waste and dirt that can damage Earth

sea stack tower or point of rock sticking up out of the sea

spit long strip of sand stretching out into the sea

tidal range measurement between sea level at high and low tide

tide change in sea level caused by the pulling force of the Moon and Sun

vertical straight up and down

Index

ML   4/10